One
Minute
Manners™

One
Minute
Manners™

Quick Solutions to the
Most Awkward Situations
You'll Ever Face at Work

Ann Marie Sabath

BROADWAY BOOKS • NEW YORK

BROADWAY

PUBLISHED BY BROADWAY BOOKS

Published in the United States by Broadway Books, an imprint of The Doubleday Broadway Publishing Group, a division of Random House, Inc., New York.

www.broadwaybooks.com

BROADWAY BOOKS and its logo, a letter B bisected on the diagonal, are trademarks of Random House, Inc.

ONE MINUTE MANNERS is a registered trademark of Ann Marie Sabath

Book design by Charles Kreloff

Library of Congress Cataloging-in-Publication Data

Sabath, Ann Marie.
    One minute manners: quick solutions to the most awkward situations
  you'll ever face at work / Ann Marie Sabath. -- 1st ed.
    p. cm.
  1. Business etiquette. I. Title
  HF5389.S234 2007
  395.5'2--dc22

                                                2006028811

ISBN 978-0-7679-2330-9

PRINTED IN THE UNITED STATES OF AMERICA

SPECIAL SALES
This title may be purchased for business or promotional use for special sales. For information, please write to: Special Markets Department, Random House, Inc., 1745 Broadway, MD 6-3, New York, NY 10019 or specialmarkets@randomhouse.com.

10 9 8 7 6 5

*This book is dedicated
to the life and memory of my father and mother,
Camille Kay and Mary Amelia Sabath.
The love, support and dedication they imparted
as parents and grandparents will live on
through their offspring.*

Contents

Acknowledgments

Writing a book appears to be an individual project, yet the reality is that it takes an entire team. I'd first like to thank my son, Scott, my daughter, Amber, and my sister, Patty, who lent me both their ears—and many scenarios for this book. I'd also like to thank my assistant, Suzy, who is my business soul.

Next, a huge thank you to Bob Sherwood, a wordsmith who inspired me to create the rudeness reduction marketing campaign for At Ease Inc.

And thanks also to Mel Parker of Mel Parker Books, who became my cohort in giving *One Minute Manners* a life of its own.

Many thanks to Charles Conrad, Executive Editor at Broadway Books, who had the vision for this project—and a special thanks to Sharon Brinkman for her insightful editing and to Charles Kreloff for his great design sense.

Finally, I am deeply grateful to my past and present At Ease Inc. workshop participants. You have inspired me by your interest in learning what it takes to climb the slippery ladder of success...and by your desire to become true professionals.

Introduction

Today's workforce is filled with intelligent, sociable, and competent people—individuals just like you. Yet many of you may have experienced moments of hesitation when confronted with how to navigate the many common awkward situations that are a daily fact of professional life. Well-educated and highly trained as you may be, I would venture to say that you've questioned how to put your best fork forward at a business meal, what to wear to a meeting when your client's dress is casual, why your organization encourages more professional dress, and how to excuse yourself from a business conversation without looking like you're cutting the other person off.

Simply put, if you'd like to advance in your career, you will want to acquire a mastery of appropriate business etiquette. You realize that knowing how to conduct yourself in the workplace can provide you with the unspoken strategies for success—which will allow you to stand out in the crowd and distinguish yourself from the competition. The business world can be a challenging environment, and learning these professional skills will give you that competitive advantage.

Yet for people entering the workplace for the first time, and even for many who are climbing that slippery ladder of success, business etiquette remains a mystery. While few universities and colleges integrate it into their curriculum, knowing "what to do and when" has emerged as a business priority, a qualitative improvement that can assist new and seasoned professionals to be more effective in business.

Business etiquette is much more than knowing which fork to use for the salad. It's a complete system of learning how to become more successful, a framework for communicating that you "get it" in a sincere, professional, and ultimately effective manner.

There are many encyclopedic books on protocol and etiquette. As a twenty-year veteran in the business etiquette arena, my objective for writing *One Minute Manners* was to provide a twenty-first-century primer on business etiquette manners for those on-the-go individuals searching for the kind of quick answers to etiquette emergencies that will label you as a polished professional.

I hope you enjoy *One Minute Manners*—and that it gives you the confidence and savoir-faire for accomplishing your professional goals.

— ANN MARIE SABATH

One
Minute
Manners™

In the
Workplace

Greetings and Introductions

Awkward Situation:
Not being able to attach a name to the face of the person approaching you.

One Minute Solution:
Simply extend your hand and say your first and last name. Better chance than not the person will mimic you—with his name, that is. However, if you definitely know the person and his name still escapes you, simply speak in general terms without using names. For example, you might say, "What's been going on since we last spoke?" General questions may trigger an answer that will bring the person's name to mind.

Actions and getting to the point speak louder than a lot of jibber-jabber. Rather than being labeled as a person who gives TMI—too much information (e.g., "I'm sorry, I'm so bad with names. I've forgotten your name. How do we know each other?")—let your handshake and name be the cues that prompt the other person to greet you using his name.

Handling the Unknown

AWKWARD SITUATION:
Wondering if you should say, "It's nice to meet you" or "It's nice to see you" when an individual greets you, making you feel as though he is a long lost friend.

ONE MINUTE SOLUTION:
When you find yourself in this awkward situation, say, "It's nice to see you." Even though this person may be unfamiliar to you, this greeting will be perceived as warmer than "It's nice to meet you." "It's nice to meet you" also implies that this is the first time you are meeting this person.

Oftentimes individuals may recognize you without you necessarily knowing them, especially if you are in a highly visible position. When you find yourself in this situation, remember it's not about you, it's about making the other person feel comfortable.

Yes, Sir

AWKWARD SITUATION:
Being unsure of how to address individuals higher in rank than you.

ONE MINUTE SOLUTION:
This varies widely based on the corporate environment. If you are being introduced to Mr. Smith, the CEO, for the first time, you should err on the side of conservative by responding, "It's nice to meet you, Mr. Smith." But on subsequent sightings of the CEO in the hallways, it is perfectly alright to say, "Good morning, how are you?" instead of the more formal "Good morning, Mr. Smith."

Meeting and Greeting: Barry, Larry, or Gary?

AWKWARD SITUATION:
Having someone greet you using the wrong name. For example, "Larry, it's good to see you."

ONE MINUTE SOLUTION:
Simply extend your hand and say your correct name: "Gary Smith. It's good to see you, too."

By extending your hand and saying your name, you're accomplishing two things: (1) you're reciprocating the greeting, and (2) you're helping the misinformed person learn your name. By handling this faux pas in a diplomatic way, you're also sparing this person the embarrassment of calling you by the wrong name throughout the conversation.

Making the Connection: Don't Make More of It Than It Is, or Move On

AWKWARD SITUATION:
Mistaking someone as a coworker's brother/roommate/friend only to learn that the person is his personal life partner.

ONE MINUTE SOLUTION:
Don't make more of it than it is. Simply say, "It's nice to meet you" followed by a point of common interest and/or the environment in which the gathering is taking place. Nothing more, nothing less. In the future, avoid assuming others' relationships.

Relationships come in many forms. You can be certain that the couple will only be as comfortable as you make them feel based on how you react to the situation.

Warm or Cold?

AWKWARD SITUATION:
Wanting to greet someone with a handshake during a cold winter day when you are wearing gloves.

ONE MINUTE SOLUTION:
If it is above freezing, slip off the glove on your right hand for a minute and shake hands. If it is below freezing, greet wearing your glove.

Although an ideal handshake is made without wearing a glove, wearing one glove is secondary to the sincere interest you display when greeting the person. You can do this by greeting her by name, smiling, and giving your full attention for the few minutes you are together.

Shaking Hands with the Person Seated Two People Away from You

AWKWARD SITUATION:
Being introduced to someone seated two people away from you.

ONE MINUTE SOLUTION:
Extend your hand only *after* standing and greeting the person behind the chair of the individual who introduced you.

Oftentimes, the individuals being introduced do the first thing that comes to mind by holding out their hands directly in front of the person next to them. Instead, as the introduction begins to take place, maintain eye contact with the person to whom you are being introduced as you stand up and offer your hand behind the seated person who has introduced the two of you. The individual to whom you are being presented will follow your lead.

Too Close for Comfort

AWKWARD SITUATION:
Receiving a hug from a client that makes you feel uncomfortable.

ONE MINUTE SOLUTION:
Take control the next time you greet the person by extending your hand with your arm straight out, then giving the person a double-hand clasp.

By extending your arm straight out, you will be creating distance between you and this hugger. A double-hand clasp will give this person a warmer greeting than a mere handshake. It also may save you from another bear hug.

Helping Others to Establish Rapport

AWKWARD SITUATION:
Wondering how you can assist people to remember each other's names after they have been introduced.

ONE MINUTE SOLUTION:
After you have made the initial introduction, make a point of using each person's name during the conversation (e.g., "Joe, Natalie represents her company's Latin American division.").

You can be sure that both individuals will appreciate you making mention of their names. Besides assisting them, they will see you as a polished professional who knows how to connect others—name and all.

When He Is She

AWKWARD SITUATION:
Receiving correspondence from someone who wrongly assumes your gender since you have a name such as Sam Barnes or Leslie Hawkins that could be used for a man or a woman.

ONE MINUTE SOLUTION:
Place a call to the person. Unless you are a woman with a very low voice or a man with a very high voice, this verbal communication should take care of it.

Generic names can indeed be confusing. You will spare the person an embarrassing moment by letting this individual discover this discrepancy by hearing your voice. If the person acknowledges the error, simply play it down by saying it happens quite frequently when communication begins through the written word.

Let's Call It a Night

AWKWARD SITUATION:
You are a woman and your male boss has had too much to drink at an office cocktail party. He asks you if you would like to join him and some others for a nightcap at the bar down the street. You are uncomfortable with this invitation and don't know how to respond.

ONE MINUTE SOLUTION:
Decline the invitation and call it a night.

Anytime you find yourself in an awkward situation such as this one, err on the side of conservative. Your job responsibilities do not include being your boss's drinking buddy. Leave it to others to help your boss drown his sorrows as you get a good night's sleep and prevent finding yourself in what could become a compromising situation.

It's a Small World after All

AWKWARD SITUATION:

You discover that someone you're now working with is an individual with whom you've had a romantic relationship in the past. How do you respond when you're reintroduced to that person at a company gathering?

ONE MINUTE SOLUTION:

Greet the person as you would anyone else. Recognize that this individual will only be as comfortable seeing you as you make it.

If you find yourself with this person for more than a mere introduction, keep your composure by asking the person about an interest that he or she shared with you when you were dating, a family member or the like. By doing so, you will be displaying your sense of confidence and also be re-framing the relationship.

Mixing Business with Pleasure

AWKWARD SITUATION:
Receiving a personal dinner invitation from a major client with a Don Juan reputation and wondering how to decline.

ONE MINUTE SOLUTION:
Rather than walking on shaky ground, thank the person for extending the invitation. Explain that you are, however, in a committed relationship.

Whether or not you are involved with another person, the best way to keep from deflating the client's ego is by saying that you are. By doing so, this client is less likely to take your "no thank you" personally.

Letting the Relationship out of the Bag

AWKWARD SITUATION:
You're involved in an office romance with a coworker, and your boss, who is not aware of this relationship, asks you both to go on a sales trip together. Knowing that this will provoke much office gossip, you wonder the best way to maintain your professional demeanor in the face of this request.

ONE MINUTE SOLUTION:
Unless you and your coworker are dating seriously, keep your personal affairs to yourself. What you do on your time is no one else's business unless it is affecting your professional productivity.

As for the gossip grapevine, ignore it. They are living vicariously through you.

Roving Eyes

AWKWARD SITUATION:
You wonder how to repent for having gotten drunk at the company holiday party and making the unforgivable error of flirting with the boss's wife.

ONE MINUTE SOLUTION:
The only thing worse than flirting with your boss's wife is confronting him about it. If you still have a job the next time you go to work, focus on making your boss look good by doing an excellent job.

It may be your only form of repentance and also the only reason your boss decides to keep you on the payroll.

Playing Political Hardball

AWKWARD SITUATION:

You receive a telephone call from the CEO telling you he's heard a lot about your good work and that he wants to take you to lunch and tell you about an exciting new job opportunity in the company. However, when you mention this to your immediate supervisor, she tells you that she's heard nothing about this.

ONE MINUTE SOLUTION:

Consider the invitation from your organization's CEO a compliment and readily accept it.

Besides being the politically correct thing to do, accepting the invitation lets the CEO know that you are interested in growing within the organization. While this new position may come as a surprise to your supervisor, worry not. You did the politically correct thing by mentioning the invitation extended to you by the CEO.

Keeping up on Downsizing Data

Awkward Situation:
You've just heard that a major downsizing is about to occur in your organization. How do you get more information?

One Minute Solution:
Keep your nose to the grindstone and ears wide open. Oftentimes, the gossip grapevine contains some facts, diluted as they may be. Remain an asset to your organization by continuing to be productive.

If you have a good relationship with your manager or human resources director, ask her to update you about how this downsizing may affect your position.

Chasing Potential Employers

Awkward Situation:
Leaving a voicemail for a potential employer and not receiving a callback.

One Minute Solution:
Wait one week, and then follow up in writing rather than by phone.

Oftentimes written follow-up communications get employers to react when voicemails don't. Be sure to mention in your correspondence that a voicemail message was left, but since you didn't receive a reply, you thought it might be best to follow up in writing. You may be surprised at how much this prospective employer appreciates your initiative.

Touchy Transpositions

AWKWARD SITUATION:
Realizing after you mailed your cover letter and resume to an employer whose first name is Alan that you mistakenly typed his name as "Anal."

ONE MINUTE SOLUTION:
Whatever you do, don't call this person to try to recover from this terrible faux pas. Instead, send a corrected letter and second resume with the word "Revised" in the upper right-hand corner of the cover letter.

Computers are only as good as the people who use them. Don't rely on spell-check or grammar-check to do the work of reviewing correspondence before it is sent. When time permits, be sure to proofread a hard copy of an important document, or set it aside for a few hours or even a day. Looking at the document with a fresh eye will make typos jump out.

Managing Unexpected Cell Phone Interruptions

AWKWARD SITUATION:
Having your cell phone ring in the middle of a job interview.

ONE MINUTE SOLUTION:
Apologize for the interruption and then switch your phone to "off" without reading the incoming number on the screen.

Cell phones should always be turned off, especially before entering a building in which a scheduled meeting will take place. Besides sparing you the embarrassment of having your cell phone go off during an important job interview, you'll be contributing to the greater good of decreased noise pollution.

Timing Is Everything

AWKWARD SITUATION:
Being asked to accept a job offer in writing within forty-eight hours when you are still waiting to hear from two other companies whose positions are of more interest to you.

ONE MINUTE SOLUTION:
If the company that has made you an offer calls, let them know that you're very pleased by their offer and will let them know your decision in a few days. In the meantime, without telling the company that has made you the offer that two other organizations are interested in you, you can call or e-mail the two other firms to tell them you have a job offer and need to respond in 48 hours.

If either of the two other companies considers you their top candidate, they will do what it takes to expedite their hiring decisions. If they do not, remember that "A bird in the hand is worth two in the bush."

Here Today, Gone Tomorrow

AWKWARD SITUATION:
Being verbally offered a job, only to learn one month later that the person who offered you the position is no longer employed there.

ONE MINUTE SOLUTION:
Contact the company and ask to speak to the hiring manager about the situation.

If you have any of your own correspondence thanking the person who made the job offer, be sure to show it. But if that gets you nowhere, be ready to pound the pavement once again, realizing the importance of getting job offers in writing in the future.

Using Good Judgment

AWKWARD SITUATION:
You've just had dinner with an important client who's had too much to drink, and he insists on driving you home. You are afraid, however, to get in the car with him.

ONE MINUTE SOLUTION:
Client or not, find another way to get home.

There are instances when other circumstances take precedence over client relationships, and this is one of them. If your relationship is strong enough to tell your client you would prefer to drive him home and then take a cab from there, do so. If you have a more distant relationship with this person, let him know that you would like to arrange a taxi for each of you and leave the car at the restaurant.

Handling Mishaps

Awkward Situation:
You're at a formal company dinner and you've spilled an entire glass of red wine all over your shirt, and it's the beginning of the evening.

One Minute Solution:
Make light of this mishap as you excuse yourself from the table. Request club soda from the bar so that you can make every attempt to blot the stain to the point that you will be able to enjoy your dinner engagement for the remainder of the evening.

The way in which you handle this spill will make others feel either at ease or uncomfortable. Rather than focusing on this mishap, divert the conversation to a topic other than the spill.

Communicate
Correctly

A Few More Bytes

AWKWARD SITUATION:
Instead of responding to an e-mail by hitting "Reply," a colleague continues to answer your inquiries by sending e-mail messages with his reply only, rather than including your question with his response, which causes you to have to refer to your original message.

ONE MINUTE SOLUTION:
The next time you request an e-mail response from this person, specifically ask that your original message be included with the reply.

While the person may believe that you have a "photographic memory" and that he is acting in a most efficient manner, he does not realize that the storage he is saving you is costing you the time to retrieve your original message.

!?&!%!

AWKWARD SITUATION:
A colleague keeps using online slang in e-mail messages to you and emphasizes points using all caps.

ONE MINUTE SOLUTION:
The golden rule also applies with e-mail manners: "Do unto others as you would have them do unto you."

Since you are not this person's manager, it's not up to you to mind his e-mail "p's and q's." Instead, your responsibility is to set the record straight by demonstrating e-mail literacy in your communication to him.

How to Follow Up

AWKWARD SITUATION:
You want to thank an interviewer for taking time to meet with you; however, you don't know whether you should write or type the thank-you letter.

ONE MINUTE SOLUTION:
When in doubt, err on the side of conservative by typing the letter of thanks. Do this within twenty-four to forty-eight hours from the time of the actual interview. If for some reason you are not able to follow up in writing within one to two days, do so as quickly as you can.

Since this communication may be shared with others who are instrumental in making the hiring decision, your typed correspondence may hold more weight by looking more professional than the handwritten one. Also, if your cursive is like a doctor's handwriting, a typed letter also will allow the interviewer to read your follow-up message rather than trying to decipher your penmanship.

Haste Makes Waste

AWKWARD SITUATION:
You've mistakenly forwarded a confidential message to the wrong person.

ONE MINUTE SOLUTION:
Send a follow-up message to the individual stating that a confidential e-mail was mistakenly sent to him. Request that the content be kept just that—confidential.

Remember, if you can reach the person as expeditiously by phone, it would be appropriate to call him and request that the message content remain confidential.

When You Don't Want to Write a Letter of Reference

AWKWARD SITUATION:
Having a former employee ask you to prepare a letter of reference to a potential employer when you are uncomfortable recommending the person.

ONE MINUTE SOLUTION:
If you know someone within the organization had a better impression of the person than you did, recommend that the former employee contact that person. Honesty is important; however, so is tact.

By suggesting that another person who has worked with the former employee send the letter of reference, both you and the person requesting the endorsement will be accomplishing your goal. Also, you will not be compromising your ethics by writing a letter of recommendation for an employee whom you would not want to recommend.

A Bit Too Informal

AWKWARD SITUATION:
Addressing someone for the first time when you have never met the person.

ONE MINUTE SOLUTION:
When writing to a person for the first time whom you have not yet met, address that individual by either "Mr." or "Ms." If the individual's name is ambiguous with respect to gender, such as Cameron, the proper form of address in writing is "Cameron Miller." When writing to government officials, clergy, and other officials with honorific titles, consult a good dictionary like Webster's, whose "Forms of Address" section provides all the rules you will need.

Your actions will speak much louder than trying to explain that you prefer the relationship remain formal. Whatever you do, avoid referring to yourself in an honorific manner by using "Mr.," "Ms.," or "Mrs."

Miss or Ms.?

AWKWARD SITUATION:
Wondering if you should use "Miss" or "Ms." when sending an invitation to a woman who is twenty years old.

ONE MINUTE SOLUTION:
The appropriate term to use with a twenty-year-old young lady is "Miss."

The term, "Miss" should be used for young women from the time they become teenagers through the age of twenty. When the person turns twenty-one, the term "Ms." should be used, unless she is married and has taken her husband's name. In that case, of course, "Mrs." would be used.

Politically Correct Titles, or the Definition of "Jr."

AWKWARD SITUATION:
Sending formal correspondence to a person who is a "Jr." after his father has passed away.

ONE MINUTE SOLUTION:
After his father's passing, the son should be referred to without the term "Jr."

The term "Jr." indicates that a son has the same full name as his father. The use of "Jr." also indicates his father is living.

How to Handle a Manager Who Is a Jokester

AWKWARD SITUATION:
Receiving jokes via e-mail from your manager that you do not find of interest.

ONE MINUTE SOLUTION:
While you certainly do not have to read them, the politically correct thing is to say nothing and continue to receive them.

Any topics that are irrelevant for work should be avoided during the business day. That includes jokes, no matter who sends them.

Slippery Fingers

Awkward Situation:
Griping to your colleague about the e-mail message your manager sent to you only to find that you mistakenly hit "Reply" rather than "Forward" and that your manager already opened it before you could retrieve it.

One Minute Solution:
Apologize to your manager and hope it is accepted.

The only thing to do in this situation is to admit to your lack of professionalism and move on. If you still have your job the following day, learn from this humiliating situation by putting these e-mail rules into practice: Cool down before ever sending an emotional message. Wait twenty-four hours before responding. Avoid sending emotional correspondence in the future.

Open at Your Own Risk

AWKWARD SITUATION:
Opening an envelope that was placed in your mailbox only to discover after you started reading it that it was not yours.

ONE MINUTE SOLUTION:
Simply jot the person to whom it belongs a note explaining that you mistakenly opened it since it was placed in your stack of mail.

Honesty is the best policy. It would be better for the person to know who mistakenly opened the mail rather than wondering who opened it—for perhaps the wrong reason. Note: If it is a million-dollar check, cash it and buy a one-way ticket to your favorite resort.

Was or Were?

AWKWARD SITUATION:
Realizing that you made a grammatical error as soon as you said it.

ONE MINUTE SOLUTION:
Reinforce what you said except this time using the correct grammar.

The last thing you say is most often the first thing that is remembered. Although you will be reinforcing what you said in order to correct the error, others listening may hear your second comment (in which you corrected yourself) as a way of emphasizing your point.

Spare Me a Card

AWKWARD SITUATION:
Receiving someone's business card only to find that you do not have one with you to give in return.

ONE MINUTE SOLUTION:
Within twenty-four to forty-eight hours of your meeting, follow up with the person in writing. Include your business card with the correspondence.

The reason business cards are exchanged is to receive another's contact information. By promptly sending a note, letter, or e-mail message to the person, you are indeed taking the initial connection to the next level of business development.

You also will be demonstrating to the person that you want to keep this business relationship alive. Note: Avoid getting caught without business cards in the future by always replenishing your card case and keeping spares close at hand.

Dealing with Misspellings

AWKWARD SITUATION:
You have discovered a misspelling in an important, time-sensitive client letter that you have already sent on behalf of your boss.

ONE MINUTE SOLUTION:
Send the corrected version to the client noting that the letter has been revised by marking it "Revised" in the upper right-hand corner of the letter.

Whether or not your boss saw the letter before it was sent, your follow-up is a direct reflection of your attention to detail.

Don't Assume

AWKWARD SITUATION:
Having someone give an explanation using an acronym with which you are unfamiliar.

ONE MINUTE SOLUTION:
When the person is at a stopping point with the explanation, ask him to clarify the acronym that was used repeating the letters you heard.

Many people assume that commonly used acronyms are common knowledge. When using acronyms, avoid assuming that everyone is familiar with them. The first time they are used during a presentation, they should be clarified, with an explanation that throughout the session, "Acme Building Corporation," for example, will be referred to as ABC.

Mark It Urgent!

AWKWARD SITUATION:

You immediately reply to a message to an entire distribution group on which you've been blind copied only to realize that you've put the sender in a jam.

ONE MINUTE SOLUTION:

Honesty is the best policy. Contact the sender immediately and ask him how he suggests you rectify this situation.

Let this be a lesson to you to think before pressing "Send." Let it also help you to see why nothing should be sent via e-mail that would be a concern if others saw it who were not meant to be copied on.

It Happens

AWKWARD SITUATION:
How to reveal that you've been inadvertently excluded from an important e-mail, which you learned about by hearing people discuss it.

ONE MINUTE SOLUTION:
Drop the person who sent the original e-mail message an e-mail message or note mentioning what you overheard. Share your involvement in the project and ask if you were supposed to be included on the distribution list. Your inquiry may jog the person's mind into remembering that you were inadvertently excluded.

Whatever you do, avoid taking it personally. Better chance than not you were mistakenly overlooked. If you find that there was a reason that you were not to get the message, don't make more of it than it is.

Using Screen Savers

AWKWARD SITUATION:
Wondering what to do when your colleague in the office next door is always reading your computer screen over your shoulder when he comes to visit.

ONE MINUTE SOLUTION:
When you see him approaching your work area, click "Save" and then close your document.

When possible, try diverting curious George's eyes when he nears your workstation. You can do this by either closing the existing document or standing up to encourage his line of vision to meet your eyes rather than your computer screen. Hopefully, this will keep his peering at your screen to a minimum when you don't want to close your document.

Sheer Embarrassment

AWKWARD SITUATION:

Wondering what to do when your boss steps into your office and catches you shopping for lingerie online. What do you say when he leers at the screen?

ONE MINUTE SOLUTION:

Close the Web page and let your boss set the tone for this most uncomfortable situation. If he does not verbalize catching you in the act, be certain that he has made a mental note. There are times that silence is golden, and this is one of them.

It's obvious that you were inappropriate in the way you were using your workday hours. Make sure it does not happen again—even when your boss is out of the office.

To Return or Not to Return

AWKWARD SITUATION:

You've forgotten to print for your boss an important document that is attached to an e-mail and you've left for the day. The only way your boss can retrieve the e-mail is if you give her your company password, and you're reluctant to give it to her.

ONE MINUTE SOLUTION:

Either give your password to your boss or go back to work and retrieve the e-mail yourself.

No matter how you look at it, the documents stored in your computer are company property.

Business
Dress
Conundrums

Teachable Moments

AWKWARD SITUATION:
You're asked to give a presentation to visiting clients on a moment's notice who are wearing suits, and your attire consists of slacks and a casual top.

ONE MINUTE SOLUTION:
Accommodate the request without apologizing for how you look. You can be certain, however, that it will not go unnoticed.

Consider this experience a teachable moment. If you find yourself in this situation once, it just may happen again. Spare yourself by keeping business professional attire at work.

How Short Is Too Short?

AWKWARD SITUATION:
You are a male manager and you are hesitant to talk to one of your female employees about her inappropriate skirt length.

ONE MINUTE SOLUTION:
Request that a female manager talk with this employee about appropriate skirt length in your work environment.

If your organization's human resources manager is a woman, ask her to address the topic with your female employee. Otherwise, request that one of your female counterparts take this person aside and have a conversation about appropriate business dress.

Work or School Day?

AWKWARD SITUATION:
Beginning a new position at a prestigious financial institution and wondering if it is appropriate to carry your belongings to work in a backpack with your university logo on it.

ONE MINUTE SOLUTION:
Begin your first day on the job with a leather portfolio and pen in hand. Based on your position, you may be given a leather or ballistic nylon computer case or other type of carrying case as part of your new employee orientation. Whatever you do, be sure to package yourself for the business setting in which you have been hired rather than looking like you are still a college student lugging a backpack.

How Casual Is Too Casual?

AWKWARD SITUATION:
You're asked to go into the office on Saturday to wrap up a project and don't know what to wear.

ONE MINUTE SOLUTION:
Wear khakis and a casual collared top or slacks and a casual top.

Each organization has a Saturday unwritten dress culture, which is based on what is worn by upper-level management. Typically, it is one notch below what is worn during the workweek. If business casual attire is worn during the week and is comprised of khakis and a casual shirt, wear that attire on Saturday. Whatever you do, avoid yard casual (e.g., what you would wear if you were mowing the lawn).

Underdressed

AWKWARD SITUATION:
You show up for a meeting with your manager and clients only to realize you are underdressed.

ONE MINUTE SOLUTION:
Make the most of the situation and learn from it.

In the future, live by the adage, "You can never get in trouble looking good." It's always better to be slightly overdressed and be able to remove a jacket or tie than it is to be underdressed and find yourself in an embarrassing situation.

Juggling the Dress Act

AWKWARD SITUATION:
You're going to an interview for a position that will require only casual wear and wonder what to wear to the interview.

ONE MINUTE SOLUTION:
Dress one notch up.

If the company defines casual wear as jeans and a t-shirt, wear khakis and an open-collared shirt to the interview. If the organization considers their workplace casual dress to be khakis and an open-collared shirt, wear a suit to the interview.

Lights, Camera, Action!

AWKWARD SITUATION:

You're preparing a presentation by videoconference and have no idea what the employees at the other company will be wearing.

ONE MINUTE SOLUTION:

When in doubt, err on the side of professionalism by wearing a suit or jacket and tie, depending on the organization's culture. In more buttoned-up conservative work environments, it is most important to follow the guideline that you can always take off a jacket if you are overdressed, but you cannot put one on if you don't have it with you. In some of the so-called glamour industries like advertising, publishing, and the media, where jackets are often not required at all, you should take the temperature of the office setting in advance and dress accordingly.

Air Dress

AWKWARD SITUATION:
You're flying to an important business meeting, and you would like to dress casually for the flight. However, you will not have time to change before the meeting.

ONE MINUTE SOLUTION:
Wear the same clothes on the flight that are appropriate for the meeting setting.

When time is of the essence between flight arrivals and scheduled meetings, it is always better to play it safe by dressing for the meeting setting.

Holey Hose!

AWKWARD SITUATION:
You are walking into a client meeting and glance down only to notice that a hole in your hosiery is extremely visible.

ONE MINUTE SOLUTION:
Ignore it.

There are times your self-confidence needs to overcome an unforeseen situation. Let this be a lesson to carry a spare pair of hosiery so that you can be more in control the next time this happens.

Backup Attire

AWKWARD SITUATION:
Renting a tuxedo for a black-tie affair only to learn as you are getting dressed that you picked up someone else's order that is two sizes too small for you.

ONE MINUTE SOLUTION:
Rather than stressing out, dress in your highest-quality black suit, starched white pointed collar shirt, black tie, and wing tips.

It's very possible that some of the men attending the function will choose to wear black suits rather than tuxedos. You should blend in well with this alternate outfit.

In the future, confirm that the order that you pick up is yours before you walk out of the store.

Mismatched

AWKWARD SITUATION:
You notice that the woman with whom you are speaking is wearing a pair of earrings (one on each ear) that do not match.

ONE MINUTE SOLUTION:
The only thing worse than wearing a pair of earrings that don't match is having it brought to your attention. Focus on what this person has to say rather than the way she has unknowingly adorned her ears.

By saying nothing about the mismatched earrings, you will keep this person from experiencing an embarrassing moment. When she does discover that she wore two different earrings, she may believe that you didn't notice since you did not make mention of it.

Talk about Good Taste!

AWKWARD SITUATION:
Going to a function only to notice that someone else is wearing the exact same designer dress as you.

ONE MINUTE SOLUTION:
Make a point of approaching the person and telling her that you like her taste.

Don't make more of the situation than it is. You can be embarrassed by this situation or make light of it. By approaching the person, you will put her, everyone at the gathering, and certainly yourself at ease.

Tongue Twister

AWKWARD SITUATION:
Having a pierced tongue and wondering if there is any reason that the adornment should be removed if it does not affect your work.

ONE MINUTE SOLUTION:
The best way to make this decision is to review your organization's policy manual in which appropriate dress is described.

Although tongue piercing might be your personal preference for accessorizing an outfit, keep your taste to yourself. Unless you see your organization's decision makers with their tongues pierced, I would recommend removing it during work hours rather than having it stick out like a sore tongue.

Underdressed

AWKWARD SITUATION:
Inviting a client to dinner at a restaurant that requires a suit coat when the person is wearing a polo shirt.

ONE MINUTE SOLUTION:
If only the two of you are going to dinner, change restaurant locations to one that is more casual.

It will be much easier to modify the location than the person's dress. If you do the reverse, your client just may mimic you by modifying his relationship with your organization.

If others will be meeting you at the establishment that requires a jacket to be worn, you have two options: (1) ask your client if you could drop him off at his home or hotel to change; or (2) call the restaurant to see if jackets are available for individuals traveling from out of town who have not packed one.

Office
Politics and
Meeting
Manners

Yawn

AWKWARD SITUATION:
Feeling yourself nod off to sleep as you are listening to a boring speaker at a meeting.

ONE MINUTE SOLUTION:
Drink water, shift positions, do anything except sleep.

Although you may be suffering from a bad night's sleep or a lack of oxygen, the last thing you want to do is insult the speaker. Get a caffeine grip or anything else that will help you display your attentiveness.

Double-Booked

AWKWARD SITUATION:
Walking into a conference room for a meeting and learning that it is being used by another group.

ONE MINUTE SOLUTION:
Do what you can to find another meeting room.

When you find yourself in this predicament, there is no sense getting upset about it. If you are spearheading the meeting, take time to find out how it occurred following the meeting. This may prevent the same situation from occurring in the future.

Hello?

Attending an in-house meeting with individuals two levels above you and not being introduced to anyone.

Create an opportunity to introduce yourself to others. For example, if you select your seat, introduce yourself to the people to your immediate left and right. If you are getting a beverage and happen to be standing next to someone, take the initiative to meet that person. When you are given the floor during the meeting, first thank the person who has put you on the agenda and then take a minute to look at each person as you say, "Good afternoon. Although a few of us have officially met, I'd like to introduce myself to everyone else. My name is Amber Wert, in XYZ position of our Corporate Marketing Department."

A savvy meeting planner should begin a meeting by introducing everyone present. When *you* are spearheading a meeting, be sure to never assume the fact that everyone has been introduced. Even if individuals have officially met, your recap of meeting participants will refresh even the memories of those who have met each other yet may be experiencing a memory lapse.

Seeing Double

AWKWARD SITUATION:
Discovering that you are double-booked as you look at your morning schedule.

ONE MINUTE SOLUTION:
Certainly call or e-mail the person spearheading one of the meetings to explain that you will have to break your commitment. Rather than leaving the person in a lurch, offer to have one of your team attend the meeting on your behalf.

To not show up without first notifying the person who invited you is plain rude. Perhaps you need to revisit your method of electronic or pen-to-paper planning.

How Long?

AWKWARD SITUATION:
You are waiting for a person who is late. How long do you wait?

ONE MINUTE SOLUTION:
If you have been waiting fifteen minutes or longer, first place a call to the person. If the person is within minutes of your agreed-upon meeting, be patient and wait. If your meeting was scheduled for thirty minutes and this person's tardiness will make you run late for your next back-to-back meeting, reschedule it.

The most important thing is to avoid being late for subsequent commitments by prolonging the meeting that started late because of a newcomer for whom you were kept waiting.

Dealing with Out-of-Turn Chatter

AWKWARD SITUATION:
Having people chat among themselves as you are addressing a group.

ONE MINUTE SOLUTION:
Stop talking completely as though you are pausing. This should wrap up the chatter.

The term "silence is golden" is often true. Your silence will probably be heard by those whose attention you are trying to get.

Meeting Latecomers

AWKWARD SITUATION:
Having people arrive late for meetings when you are spearheading them.

ONE MINUTE SOLUTION:
Unless you are waiting for your manager or a client, begin meetings promptly.

Individuals who begin meetings late are perceived as condoning latecomers' actions. When the situation allows you to begin meetings without everyone present, do so. Close the door when the meeting is about to begin. Some managers have even been known to lock the door at the time of the scheduled meeting and not let latecomers on their team participate. This strategy has proven to be a foolproof method for getting latecomers to arrive at meetings early.

Ah, Shucks!

AWKWARD SITUATION:
Having a colleague use profanity during a meeting.

ONE MINUTE SOLUTION:
Move on.

By acknowledging the inappropriate comments, you are also giving attention to this lack of vocabulary. Behavior modification dictates that you focus on positive actions rather than on emotional outbursts that might have occurred from a lack of self-control or as an attention-getting device.

Steering a Conversation

AWKWARD SITUATION:
Having someone begin a conversation when you don't have time to talk.

ONE MINUTE SOLUTION:
Acknowledge what the person said in your own words and then schedule a mutually beneficial time that will work.

Even when you don't have time to get involved in a lengthy conversation, it is still important to acknowledge what you heard with an "I'll be in my office today from 3:00 P.M. to 5:30 P.M. and during the mornings for the rest of the week. How about if you let me know the thirty-minute blocks of time that will work with your schedule this week? I'll get back to you by the end of the day so that we can firm up a time to meet."

Grapevine Gossip

Awkward Situation:
Having a colleague speak negatively about another person whom you happen to like.

One Minute Solution:
Recommend that the person schedule a time to discuss his or her concerns with the individual who happens to be the topic of the conversation.

Lending an ear to gossip is as inappropriate as saying it yourself. By recommending that the person direct the conversation to the individual being discussed, you will be encouraging the person to handle conflicts head-on rather than circumventing the issue by discussing it with others.

Lend Me Your Ear

AWKWARD SITUATION:
Having one of your fellow employees share her tales of woe about her unhappy marriage.

ONE MINUTE SOLUTION:
Acknowledge the emotional pain that this person is experiencing by saying, "It sounds like you have gone through a lot."

Ask the person what you can do to best weather what appears to be her personal storm. By listening at an arms-length distance (in order to avoid hearing a daily saga), you are doing your due diligence as a colleague and yet distancing yourself from becoming this employee's marriage counselor.

Caller ID Etiquette

AWKWARD SITUATION:
Seeing your colleague's number on caller ID and greeting him informally when you pick up the phone only to find out that it is his boss.

ONE MINUTE SOLUTION:
Recover quickly with an "excuse me."

In the future, avoid "assuming" that the name appearing on the caller ID screen will also be the caller.

Just the Messenger

Awkward Situation:
Taking a telephone message for your boss from someone who is having trouble getting a return call from her.

One Minute Solution:
Tell the caller you will personally get the message to your boss, emphasizing that this is the caller's third request for a return call.

Based on the relationship that you have with your boss and the caller (e.g., you may handle the call differently if the person is a client versus a vendor), ask your boss what you may do to return the call to the person. Also, learn from your boss how you should treat the call if the person follows up by phone within a few days and has not received a call-back. In either case, encourage the caller to leave a message directly on your boss's voice mail so that you get and stay out of this loop.

Out of the Office

AWKWARD SITUATION:
Being away from the office for the day and knowing that you will not be able to return voice mail messages.

ONE MINUTE SOLUTION:
When you know you will be away from your work area for more than a few hours, update your message to reflect when callers can expect to hear from you.

Voice mail is the best thing since the invention of sliced bread when used properly. By updating your voice mail message, callers will hear more than "I'm not available."

A personalized voice mail message will let callers know when you will be accessible. Your updated message also will minimize the chance for prospects to give their business to your competitors.

When Professionalism Overrules Friendship

AWKWARD SITUATION:
You accidentally overhear your boss discussing the termination of your best friend with another manager.

ONE MINUTE SOLUTION:
See no evil, hear no evil. As a professional, it is only good ethics to not discuss what you heard.

While you owe loyalty to your friend, the conversation was not directed at you. For that reason, you should not repeat what you heard. Otherwise, you might be in the unemployment line too.

Temper Tantrums

Awkward Situation:
You lose your temper and respond inappropriately.

One Minute Solution:
Extend your apologies to anyone you may have offended.

While this situation may have brought out the darker side of you, the way you handle it is what will be remembered. Regain your composure, acknowledging that you let the situation control you rather than controlling the situation.

Cubicle Germs

AWKWARD SITUATION:
You want to encourage the person with whom you share office space to go home when he is sneezing and coughing to the point of potentially making you and everyone around him sick.

ONE MINUTE SOLUTION:
Unless you are the company nurse, the person's mother, or his manager, mind your business. Instead, increase your vitamin C intake and focus on your work.

In his ailing condition, this person probably wants to be at work less than you want to have him there. It is possible that this person is on a deadline or has used up his sick days. If the person's kerchoos really bother you, schedule meetings for yourself out of the office or in a vacant conference room.

Press One to Speak with a Human Being

Awkward Situation:
Having a client insist that he would prefer to leave a telephone message with you rather than in the voice mail box of the person who can handle the situation.

One Minute Solution:
Since the client is always right, tell him that you would be happy to take the message and that you will then put it directly in the voice mail box of the person who handles that matter. Before you end the telephone call, give the client the name and telephone number of the person who will be receiving this information for future reference.

Respecting Others' Space

AWKWARD SITUATION:
Wanting to make a telephone call on your cell phone without disturbing the airspace of those around you.

ONE MINUTE SOLUTION:
If you are in a room, leave. If you are in a public location, try to find an area where you can create a two-arms-length distance from those around you. Turn your back away from the people in your presence so they will not be plagued by your conversation.

By creating at least four feet between you and the others in your midst, you will be displaying a respect for the individuals around you.

A Loan without Interest

AWKWARD SITUATION:
Money is being collected for an associate's new baby gift. One of your colleagues asks if you will put in five dollars for him and he will repay you. Two weeks pass and you still haven't received the money.

ONE MINUTE SOLUTION:
Either drop your associate a note with a gentle reminder of the loan or consider it your charitable donation.

Anytime you lend money, don't expect a repayment.

Dining
Dilemmas

Eye Contact, Anyone?

AWKWARD SITUATION:
Letting a server know you are the person hosting the meal.

ONE MINUTE SOLUTION:
When the server first approaches your table, simply take charge by greeting her on behalf of the others at the table. After you greet the server, the menus have been read, and everyone is ready to order, you should then say, "I'd like my guests to go first."

Taking the initiative to greet the server accomplishes three purposes: (1) It makes it known to the server that you will be taking care of the bill. (2) It is a confirmation to guests that the meal will be your treat. (3) It lets the server know that your order should be taken last.

En el Nombre del Padre

AWKWARD SITUATION:
Wanting to say grace at a business meal.

ONE MINUTE SOLUTION:
Unless you have been asked to give the invocation, nonchalantly glance down at the food and bless it yourself in silence.

Like politics and sex, religion is one of the three topics that should not be discussed in business. Blessing your food falls into the religion category. Keep your personal preference for displaying your nourishment gratitude to yourself.

Fussy Eater

AWKWARD SITUATION:
Being served food at an evening banquet that you cannot eat because of health or religious reasons.

ONE MINUTE SOLUTION:
Try to avoid putting yourself in this situation by taking a proactive approach and letting the person inviting you know of your special dietary restrictions. If you find yourself in this situation, eat what you can. You can always grab something on the way home from the banquet.

No Moos Is Good for Vegetarians

AWKWARD SITUATION:
Being unsure of what to order at a steakhouse when you are a vegetarian and do not see an entree on the menu that will accommodate your food preference.

ONE MINUTE SOLUTION:
When it is your turn to place your order, simply ask the server, "What do you recommend for a vegetarian?"

The most important guideline for vegetarians eating at steakhouses is to play down your vegetarian preference. Instead, keep in mind that you are there for the people first and then the food.

The Mirror Effect

AWKWARD SITUATION:
Dining with someone you just met who ate a piece of food that did not completely make it into his mouth.

ONE MINUTE SOLUTION:
Blot your mouth with a napkin and hope the other person will do the same.

Whether consciously or subconsciously, people tend to mimic what others do—especially during meals. Rather than embarrassing the person by telling him that he has a piece of linguini hanging out of his mouth, hope that your blotting gesture will give him a clue.

Buffet Etiquette

AWKWARD SITUATION:
Being ready to return to the buffet table for seconds when you are the guest.

ONE MINUTE SOLUTION:
Wait for the person hosting the meal to ask you to join him/her for seconds.

It's not your last supper! Remember—people first and then the food.

Pass on the Rolls

AWKWARD SITUATION:
Having the person to your left use your bread and butter plate.

ONE MINUTE SOLUTION:
This may be your low-carb meal of the day. Forgo a roll.

If you know the person to your left quite well, you could tease him by saying, "Thank you, I love rye" when he mistakenly places his roll on your bread and butter plate.

If the person to your right has already claimed his bread and butter plate, place your roll on the side of your salad or main course plate.

If the meal is more formal in nature, avoid eating a roll. Simply stop at a bakery on the way back to work.

Oops!

AWKWARD SITUATION:
Spilling a beverage on a guest seated next to you.

ONE MINUTE SOLUTION:
Apologize as you help the person recover from the unexpected spill.

Follow up the luncheon with a note to the person and include a gift certificate to a dry cleaner in the area.

What Can I Give You toward the Bill?

AWKWARD SITUATION:

Your boss has invited you and another associate to lunch. When the bill arrives, your boss makes no attempt to pay for it.

ONE MINUTE SOLUTION:

Focus on the conversation at hand and leave the bill to your boss.

Typically, whoever extends the invitation picks up the bill. If it looks like your boss is not going to spring for the bill, casually ask, "What can I give you toward the bill?"

Chewy Conversations

AWKWARD SITUATION:
Going out to lunch with someone who talks with food in his mouth.

ONE MINUTE SOLUTION:
Minimize this gross act by asking the person questions between bites.

By waiting until the person is between bites, you are more likely to get a complete answer rather than a mouthful of food to go with it. Be sure that you are never described as the person who indulges in chewy conversations.

Off Course

AWKWARD SITUATION:
Having a server in a casual restaurant bring out the main course when you and your guests are only half finished with your salads.

ONE MINUTE SOLUTION:
Ask the server if she can return the entrees to the kitchen and bring them back in a few minutes.

This will keep your guests from feeling as though they are being rushed.

Antioxidants, Anyone?

AWKWARD SITUATION:
Your client asks if you would mind sitting in the smoking section of the restaurant so that he can smoke.

ONE MINUTE SOLUTION:
Thank your client for being considerate enough to ask and state your preference.

By asking for your seating preference, your client is demonstrating his consideration that smoke may bother you. Be candid by explaining that you would appreciate being seated in the nonsmoking area. Let your client know how much you appreciate his sensitivity in this matter.

When to Put Your Best Fork Forward

AWKWARD SITUATION:

Wondering when it is appropriate to begin eating during a meal.

ONE MINUTE SOLUTION:

Protocol dictates that guests wait for the person hosting the meal to take the first bite.

This rule began before refrigeration. If the person hosting the meal took the first bite it meant that the meal was safe.

Toasting When You Don't Drink

AWKWARD SITUATION:
Participating in a meal in which a toast is being proposed when you don't drink.

ONE MINUTE SOLUTION:
Join in the toast by lifting the beverage that you have in front of you.

What matters most is that you have a goblet or glass in front of you to raise. The host and other guests will not care what you are drinking as long as you are participating in the toast.

Hosting with a Toast

AWKWARD SITUATION:
You are hosting a meal and a toast is being proposed to you by your guests and you are wondering when you should lift your goblet.

ONE MINUTE SOLUTION:
Wait until after the toast has been completed and then propose a toast in return.

If you lift your goblet when the toast is being proposed to you, it would be as though you were singing "Happy Birthday" to yourself or applauding yourself.

Higher or Lower?

AWKWARD SITUATION:
Hosting a meal with clients and wondering if your goblet should be lower or higher than their glasses.

ONE MINUTE SOLUTION:
When toasting, your goblet always should be lower than the clients' glasses.

By having your goblet lower than your clients' glasses, you are displaying corporate deference. While it is appropriate to lift your goblet slightly higher than someone who reports to you, it may be perceived as one-upmanship. Better to keep the goblet level as a way of demonstrating that you are one of the team rather than risk being perceived as though you are on a hierarchy ego trip.

Restaurant Restrictions

AWKWARD SITUATION:
Hosting a meal only to realize that your guest keeps kosher.

ONE MINUTE SOLUTION:
Thank the person for letting you know and ask the maitre d' for a recommendation.

Make this situation a learning experience for future dining invitations by asking guests ahead of time if they have specific dietary restrictions.

Wine, Anyone?

AWKWARD SITUATION:
Hosting a dinner function when you have no clue about how to order wine.

ONE MINUTE SOLUTION:
Either defer the wine selection to the sommelier or to one of your guests who you know is a wine connoisseur.

When in doubt, delegate. Remember, it's not about the situation; it's about how it is handled.

Dom Pérignon, Anyone?

AWKWARD SITUATION:
Deferring your wine selection to a guest who orders a one-hundred-dollar bottle of wine that you know will be challenged on your expense report.

ONE MINUTE SOLUTION:
Rather than letting this unexpected situation alter your mood, enjoy both your guest's company and the wine.

If this person sends you sufficient business to merit a pricey bottle of wine, join in the celebration by taking your mind off what is being spent. Focus on the relationship at hand and let the wine flow—be cognizant, however, of the fact that your boss might not be happy seeing a one-hundred-dollar bottle of wine on the expense report. You might have to pay for this one yourself.

Bad Tippers

AWKWARD SITUATION:
Noticing that the person hosting the meal at one of your favorite restaurants left a miserly tip.

ONE MINUTE SOLUTION:
After you and your host leave the table, act as though you forgot something where you were seated and supplement the bad tip.

All of our reputations precede us. If you or someone in your organization expects to return to the restaurant, the kind of tip you leave today will determine how you will be treated at that establishment in the future.

There Is No Such Thing as a Free Lunch

AWKWARD SITUATION:
Using a "buy one get one free" meal gift certificate or coupon at a restaurant and then wondering who gets the free meal.

ONE MINUTE SOLUTION:
Both you and your friend should split the cost of the bill.

If your friend had not agreed to go to lunch in the first place, you would not have been able to use the gift certificate. Be happy that you are benefiting from both the "two-for-one" certificate and the person's company. Note: Be sure to tip on the full amount of what the meals would have been if you had not had the two-for-one coupon.

If you are on a date and are using a "buy one get one free" lunch coupon, you certainly will not impress the person to whom you are attracted. In fact, you may be giving yourself the reputation of being the last of the big spenders, and you could find yourself eating your next meal alone.

Excuse Me

Awkward Situation:

You are out to dinner with key prospective clients and the service is abominable. At one point, as the server presents the entrée to you, the plate slips out of his hand and the pasta you ordered spills all over your lap. How do you handle it?

One Minute Solution:

Rather than gritting your teeth in anger, or worse, yelling at the server, keep your composure. While the server and the rest of the waitstaff scurry around to clean up the mess, you can even lighten the moment by telling the server that your wife never liked that suit anyway and that she'll be thrilled. Then, after you excuse yourself to go to the restroom, share your dissatisfaction with the manager on duty, but above all, avoid complaining about the service to your guests. Simply resolve the situation.

In the future, be sure to select restaurants known for both excellent cuisine and superior service. And, more importantly, in this kind of situation never scream at the server or the manager in front of your guests. By handling this scenario with ease rather than arrogance, condescension, and anger, you will demonstrate both good character and your ability to handle stressful work situations in a similar manner.

Overcoming Financial Indigestion

AWKWARD SITUATION:

You are out of town and having dinner with clients. You pick up the tab; however, you are told by the server that your credit card has been declined. It is the only one that you have with you, and you do not have enough cash to pay for the meal.

ONE MINUTE SOLUTION:

Thank the server for letting you know there is a problem. Then excuse yourself from the table and explain the situation to the restaurant manager as you hand her your business card. If you have patronized this restaurant in the past, the management may work with you either by billing you or arranging for another form of payment the following day.

If you are traveling to a city where you rarely do business, however, or are in an environment unlike where you normally host meals, your credit card company may question if the charge is fraudulent. On the other hand, if your credit card has been declined because payment is overdue, learn to better manage your financial affairs.

When You Have to Ask a Client to Take Care of the Bill

AWKWARD SITUATION:
You're out with a client in another city, and you realize you've left your wallet and credit cards in the hotel room safe. How do you pay for dinner?

ONE MINUTE SOLUTION:
Ask your client if he will spare you an embarrassing moment with the establishment by picking up the bill.

Be sure to request a copy of the bill so that you can get a personal check to your client within twenty-four to forty-eight hours of this dining dilemma.

Social
Events

Juggling Appetizers and Drinks

AWKWARD SITUATION:

Trying to juggle an appetizer plate and a goblet in your left hand so that your right hand is free to shake hands.

ONE MINUTE SOLUTION:

If you feel like an official juggler as you are trying to manage both items, choose to carry either the glass or the appetizer plate.

Many people act like the reception table is a mini-dinner. What should be remembered, however, is that the food and beverage are secondary to the real reason for getting together. The focus of the evening should be to become acquainted with other guests.

To Open or Not to Open

AWKWARD SITUATION:
Not being sure if you should open a business gift in front of the person who gave it to you.

ONE MINUTE SOLUTION:
Avoid opening the gift unless the person encourages you to do so.

While most Americans tear open the wrappings within minutes of receiving a gift, it is considered rude in many cultures. The reason: If you are exchanging gifts with others and your gift is of higher value, it could embarrass the giver.

Not Having a Gift Acknowledged

AWKWARD SITUATION:
Not receiving a "thank you" for a gift sent via U.S. mail one month ago and wondering whether the person ever received it.

ONE MINUTE SOLUTION:
The next time you talk with the person, ask if it has been received.

If the person does not have "the smarts" to send a thank you, it certainly would be considered appropriate for you to confirm that it indeed has been received.

An Unwelcome Gift

AWKWARD SITUATION:
Receiving a gift from a guest who apparently does not know your taste.

ONE MINUTE SOLUTION:
Thank the person for being thoughtful rather than for the gift itself.

Maintain a positive perspective by remembering that it is the thought that counts rather than the gift itself. Rather than fibbing by sharing how much you like the gift, express your appreciation to the person for remembering you on the occasion for which the gift is being sent.

An After-the-Fact Gift

Awkward Situation:
Going to a gathering at someone's home without a gift in hand.

One Minute Solution:
Send a gift the following day to accompany the thank-you note.

While candy, nuts, or wine make great gifts when they are in hand, a gift sent the following day should reflect the taste of the person's home or family's interests.

When an RSVP Turns into a Regret

AWKWARD SITUATION:
You have sent in your RSVP to a sit-down dinner in someone's home only to forget about it the day it takes place.

ONE MINUTE SOLUTION:
As soon as you realize your faux pas, call the person and express your sincere regret for missing the gathering. Follow up by sending a gift expressing your disappointment about not being able to share in the event.

While to err is human, it sounds like you may need to revamp your system for keeping commitments. Review your planner to see what you can do to prevent engagements from slipping through the cracks in the future.

Going That Extra Mingle

AWKWARD SITUATION:
You are talking with someone at an unstructured gathering and want to continue to work the room. You feel uncomfortable leaving the person, considering she just mentioned that she knows no one at the event.

ONE MINUTE SOLUTION:
Transition your departure from this person by first introducing her to someone you know.

Most people find it uncomfortable to enter a roomful of strangers. Since this person seems to fall in this category, your "Good Samaritan" deed of introducing her to someone else before moving on will be much appreciated.

RSVP

Awkward Situation:
Sending invitations that require an RSVP and only hearing from fifteen of the twenty guests.

One Minute Solution:
Contact the individuals who have not responded to find out their decision.

This lack of follow-through is by far one of the greatest business/social faux pas. Individuals extending invitations should never interpret a lack of response as meaning that these invitees will not be attending the gathering. The person following up with the individuals who did not respond may be surprised to learn how many were planning to attend the function even though they did not *répondez s'il vous plaît.*

How Early Is Too Early?

AWKWARD SITUATION:
Having a guest show up two hours early for a party.

ONE MINUTE SOLUTION:
Invite the individual into your home. Mention that the gathering does not begin for another two hours and welcome the person to make himself at home.

While you don't want to make the person feel any more uncomfortable than he is by showing up early, your mention that other guests are scheduled in two hours may be a tactful way of encouraging the person to leave and return at the appropriate time. If the person prefers to stay and is a friend, take advantage of having another pair of hands by putting the person to work helping with those last-minute party preparations.

Lights Out!

AWKWARD SITUATION:
You have a power outage as your party is about to begin.

ONE MINUTE SOLUTION:
Go with the flow. Make it a candlelight dinner.

This unplanned circumstance will be received only as well as you handle it. In fact, when having a dinner party, keep candles close at hand in case this unlikely situation ever occurs.

Delegating Responsibilities When Hosting a Meal

AWKWARD SITUATION:
You are hosting a meal and you choose to avoid alcohol, yet you know your guests would like wine.

ONE MINUTE SOLUTION:
Ask a guest who you know enjoys wine with dinner to do the honors.

By deferring the wine selection to a guest who is known for having wine savvy, you will be displaying your skill at being a gracious host rather than showing yourself to be a person who is known for focusing on his beverage preferences.

Shhh!

AWKWARD SITUATION:
Having the people sitting in back of you talk while you are trying to listen to a speaker.

ONE MINUTE SOLUTION:
Let a turn of your head, facial expression, or your index finger on your lips be signs for asking these talkers to be quiet.

Your body language should be sufficient for telling the individuals that their chatter is annoying. If that doesn't work, quietly tell these individuals that their talking is keeping you from hearing the speaker.

How to Unload a Bore

AWKWARD SITUATION:
We've all been there. You find yourself engaged in a conversation with someone and are trying to get away without offending that person.

ONE MINUTE SOLUTION:
Whether you are talking with a charismatic or boring individual, follow this rule: as you begin to disengage, prepare to shake the person's hand while referring to a comment that he or she shared with you earlier. For example, "George, it's been nice talking with you. I hope you enjoy your upcoming trip to Tokyo."

This exit strategy is definitely more appropriate than pretending you need to excuse yourself to refresh your drink or use the restroom or looking at your watch and making a comment about needing to talk to a few others in the room.

Ready, Set, Mingle

AWKWARD SITUATION:
Feeling uncomfortable when you enter a roomful of strangers at a business reception.

ONE MINUTE SOLUTION:
Before you enter a roomful of strangers, position yourself as a person with a purpose by creating a mingling strategy.

The main reason many people feel uncomfortable attending receptions is the lack of structure. Savvy networkers, however, map out a mental agenda before they attend functions. Their mission can include approaching three people they don't know, exchanging business cards when appropriate, acknowledging people they do know, and then leaving the gathering at a specific time.

Happy Holidays

AWKWARD SITUATION:
Wishing someone a "Merry Christmas" only to learn that the person celebrates Hanukah.

ONE MINUTE SOLUTION:
When unsure of another's religious practices, play it safe with "Happy Holidays" as the greeting.

We live in a diverse society, and sensitivity to holiday greetings should reflect just that. When you know that someone celebrates Christmas, a "Merry Christmas!" is great. Otherwise, bid others holiday cheer with a generic greeting.

Travel
Manners

Driving Protocol

Awkward Situation:

You and your boss are traveling by car to a conference that is six hours away, and you are wondering if you should offer to drive.

One Minute Solution:

Prior to beginning your road trip, offer to take over the driver's seat at any time during the trip. Let your boss take it from there.

If your boss wants you to drive, he will let you know. Otherwise, assume the role of navigator if you are offered a map. Whatever you do, avoid the role of a "backseat driver."

Respecting Airspace

AWKWARD SITUATION:

You're traveling by plane with one of your associates and you know that you are going to have to discuss business on the flight. You're both given aisle seats across from each other.

ONE MINUTE SOLUTION:

Ask one of the persons seated in the middle next to either of you if he would switch a middle seat for one of your aisle seats.

Most people would be thrilled to have an aisle seat both for convenience and for legroom. If your request is not accepted, delay your business conversation until after you have arrived at your destination and have deplaned.

Be Prepared to Pay

AWKWARD SITUATION:
You and your boss are traveling on business, and you get out of the taxi at the hotel. The driver waits for his fare and tip. Who pays?

ONE MINUTE SOLUTION:
If your boss does not get out his wallet as the taxi arrives at your destination, take care of the fare and tip.

Always be prepared to pay by carrying ample expense money. Either way, it doesn't really matter who pays since it will either be on your expense report or your boss's.

Beyond the Job Description

AWKWARD SITUATION:
After a long day at work, you are sitting next to your boss on a flight. She dozes off to sleep and unknowingly rests her head on your shoulder.

ONE MINUTE SOLUTION:
Casually shift your body. This movement may realign her sleeping position.

Lending your shoulder is a little too close for comfort. You will be doing both yourself and your boss a favor by shifting your weight.

When Hal Is Seated Next to You

AWKWARD SITUATION:
The person on the plane next to you has a bad case of halitosis.

ONE MINUTE SOLUTION:
After you visit with the individual for a few minutes, nonchalantly take out your breath freshener mints and offer one to the person.

If that doesn't work, maintain your cordiality until everyone has boarded and been seated. At that point, arrange to move to an available seat mentioning to the person that your move will give him more legroom.

Now What?

AWKWARD SITUATION:
Boarding a plane only to see that someone else is sitting in your assigned seat.

ONE MINUTE SOLUTION:
Compare seat assignments with the person.

If he has mistakenly taken your seat and has already settled in it, take his assigned seat if it is comparable. If your assigned seat is on an aisle and the person's assigned seat is the middle, tell him that you'll be happy to wait until he packs up.

Lending an Ear

ORDINARY SITUATION:

AWKWARD SITUATION:
The person seated on the flight next to you has the gift of gab, and you don't particularly want to talk.

ONE MINUTE SOLUTION:
Be cordial as you encourage the conversation to come to an end by not adding to what the person said.

By not continuing the conversation, you will be tactfully throwing the hint that you would like the time in the air to yourself. Pulling out a book or paperwork or preparing to take a power nap also may help to drop the "I would like time to myself" hint.

When a Casanova Joe Is Seated Next to You

AWKWARD SITUATION:
Your fellow passenger appears to be hitting on you during a transoceanic flight.

ONE MINUTE SOLUTION:
Bring up your spouse or long-term relationship during the course of the conversation.

Keep your composure while you are on the flight by maintaining control of the conversation. Change the subject when necessary, sleep, etc. Once you deplane, you'll be home free from this person.

First or Coach?

AWKWARD SITUATION:
You are traveling by plane with your client and only your seat has been upgraded to first class.

ONE MINUTE SOLUTION:
Discreetly ask the gate agent to reassign your upgraded seat to your client.

Eating crow, I mean pretzels or peanuts, will be well worth the effort of having your client treated to first-class service. Some gate agents may even seat both of you in first class if additional seats are available.

Overindulging in Midnight Snacks

AWKWARD SITUATION:

You realize as you are about to check out of the hotel that you've virtually emptied the minibar in your room and your company is about to be charged $411.00. What do you do?

ONE MINUTE SOLUTION:

Pay for your overindulgence out of your own pocket.

Costly lessons often are remembered, and this should be one of them. The last thing you want to do is be perceived by your organization as being wasteful with their money.

Don't Leave Home without It

Awkward Situation:
You're at dinner in Mumbai with two clients, and you realize that you've contracted a gastrointestinal disorder that prevents you from spending more than five minutes at a time at the table. How do you handle this?

One Minute Solution:
Slip the manager the equivalent of twenty dollars and request that he ask someone to go to the closest apothecary to pick up a medicine such as Lomotil for you.

During future international trips, keep the necessary tablets with you to prevent being in this situation.

Good Shot

AWKWARD SITUATION:
You've been asked to play golf with your boss and an important client next week; however, you don't know how to play golf. How do you respond?

ONE MINUTE SOLUTION:
Tell your boss that you'd like to take a rain check on this invitation. Explain that you have not yet taken up the sport.

Treat this invitation as a stimulus for scheduling golf lessons so that you are prepared to accept future invitations. Make a point of scheduling weekly lessons and remember: avid golfers know that it never rains on the golf course.

Calling All Cars

AWKWARD SITUATION:
You're out with clients at a nightclub in what you come to realize is the wrong part of town. It's late, there are no taxis, the establishment has closed, and you're all stranded.

ONE MINUTE SOLUTION:
When all else fails, call a cab company to get you back to your hotel. If you are in a small city or town that does not support taxis, call the police and ask them for a lift.

Learn from the situation by having a say in choosing clubs more wisely in the future. Also, make a point of calling it a night earlier the next time rather than "closing down the house." This way you may have easier access to transportation to your hotel.

International
Etiquette
Emergencies

A Mirror Image

AWKWARD SITUATION:
You're meeting a prospective Japanese client for the first time and don't know whether you should shake hands or bow.

ONE MINUTE SOLUTION:
Wait to see how your client greets you and then follow suit.

If your Japanese client extends his hand, be sure that you stand two arms lengths from the person and that your handshake is a light, lingering one.

If your client bows, be sure to do the same, lowering your eyes as you bend. If you are a woman, keep your hands in front of you with palms down. As you bend, slide your hands from your thighs to your knees keeping your head lower than your Japanese client. Men should do the same; except their hands should remain at their sides as they greet with the bow.

Touch of the Heart

AWKWARD SITUATION:
You're having a dim sum lunch with Chinese clients and you are famished. You would like to begin eating but you don't know if it is permissible.

ONE MINUTE SOLUTION:
Wait until everyone has been served by the person to their left or right.

A dim sum (which means "touch of the heart") meal is a shared experience during breakfast or lunch settings. After the food selected by the host has been placed on the revolving tray, you will be served one food by your host. You also will be expected to serve the host in return. As you finish the piece of food using your chopsticks, of course, you will be served another item by your host. Be sure to reciprocate.

Gift-Giving Protocol

AWKWARD SITUATION:
You're invited to a client's home in Hong Kong and wonder what to take as a gift.

ONE MINUTE SOLUTION:
Select an item made in your homeland that could not be bought in Hong Kong.

A coffee-table book describing your city or an item made in your country would be appropriate. If your gift is comprised of a few items, focus on giving gifts to your Hong Kong Chinese clients in threes, eights, and nines since they are considered lucky numbers. Avoid gifts in multiples of four since this is considered an unlucky number. Clocks and sharp items such as letter openers should be avoided since they signify bad luck.

Punctuality Is Key

AWKWARD SITUATION:
You arrive at a meeting in Frankfurt fifteen minutes late and are met with icy stares from your German business associates.

ONE MINUTE SOLUTION:
Learn from the reaction by being punctual for future meetings.

Structure and order are very important parts of the German culture. One way that Germans adhere to this order is by respecting others' time and certainly expecting the same in return.

Eating Counterclockwise

AWKWARD SITUATION:

You are having dinner with clients in Monaco and have been given a dirty look by your client as you are enjoying *fromage,* a plate containing a selection of cheese for dessert.

ONE MINUTE SOLUTION:

If your client also is enjoying *fromage,* notice the manner in which it is being eaten.

Form should be followed when enjoying *fromage.* The cheese placed on your plate in the six o'clock position should be tasted first. As you continue to enjoy the cheese, do so by tasting the cheese to the immediate right of the first cheese.

Continue in a counterclockwise position. The reason? The cheese has been placed on your plate from the most mild to the strongest and should be enjoyed in that fashion.

Mind Your Words

AWKWARD SITUATION:
You're at dinner with a British client and after a few glasses of wine, you begin asking questions about his family and personal life. You are met with stony silence.

ONE MINUTE SOLUTION:
Mind your consumption by switching your beverage selection to one that is nonalcoholic.

The British both stand and converse at an arms-length distance. By asking questions about your British client's personal life, you are considered to be invading the person's privacy. Play it safe during future business/social encounters by sticking to the conversation based on the subjects brought up by your client.

Patience Is a Virtue

AWKWARD SITUATION:
You're waiting in a restaurant in India for your business associate to arrive. He is already a half hour late and you're tempted to call his office to find out what is going on.

ONE MINUTE SOLUTION:
Be patient and keep waiting.

In many cultures, time is considered fluid, and that includes arriving at appointed times according to what was agreed upon. If this is the first time you have met with this client, your telephone call may act as a confirmation that the person is familiar with the restaurant location rather than reminding the person of the original time that you had agreed to meet.

Get with the Program

AWKWARD SITUATION:
Being invited to a Japanese restaurant and realizing that everyone except you appears proficient at using chopsticks.

ONE MINUTE SOLUTION:
When in Rome, do as the Romans do. Try your best to use chopsticks.

Form is a very important part of the Japanese culture. By making an effort to enjoy your meal using chopsticks, you also will be displaying your adaptability, which is a much-valued trait for developing and maintaining business relationships.

Slurping Away

AWKWARD SITUATION:

You have an Asian coworker who has been transferred from your company's Shanghai office. You have noticed that during business lunches and dinners, his table manners are very cultural, such as slurping his soup.

ONE MINUTE SOLUTION:

If you have a good personal relationship with this individual, talk to him in private about the appropriate Western style for sipping soup.

The manner in which you approach your Asian employee will be as essential as what you say. It is very important to help this individual to save face as he learns what it takes for conducting business during meals.

When Scheduling an End Time Is Offensive

AWKWARD SITUATION:
Inviting Colombian friends to your office for a Thursday evening business reception from 6:00 P.M. to 8:00 P.M. and learning that they did not attend because they were offended that the invitation stated the time the gathering would end.

ONE MINUTE SOLUTION:
Call to apologize that you unknowingly offended them. Explain that in North America, it is commonplace to state both a beginning and an end time for business/social receptions.

In the Latin American culture, stating an end time can be interpreted as meaning that the conversation that is taking place at the designated end time is less important than the appointed end time of the function.

When It Is Considered Evening

Wondering when to use *bon soir* rather than *bon jour* to greet a Frenchman.

When the clock strikes 6:00 P.M., the term *bon soir* should be used.

The term *bon jour* means both "good morning" and "good afternoon." *Bon soir*, however, means "good evening," which is considered by the French to begin at 6:00 P.M.

I Want My Coffee

AWKWARD SITUATION:
Receiving a strange look from a server in an Italian restaurant when you order a cappuccino after dinner.

ONE MINUTE SOLUTION:
When dining and choosing to have coffee after dinner, follow the proper protocol by ordering an espresso.

Coffee protocol outside the United States dictates that you order cappuccino or latte before noon. Espresso is to be taken after noon.

Am I That Boring?

AWKWARD SITUATION:
Wondering what to do when you are delivering a presentation to your Japanese clients and one of them closes his eyes and then covers them with his right hand.

ONE MINUTE SOLUTION:
Don't take it personally. Your Japanese client is covering his eyes because he is concentrating on what you are saying. If you are delivering your presentation in English, your Japanese client(s) is hearing the information in what might be considered his second language. This makes it more important to understand what is being said. Be sure to have documentation so that your international clients can also follow along by reading what you are explaining.

Why Does He Keep Replenishing My Beverage?

Awkward Situation:
Wondering why your Taiwanese client continues to top off your beverage during a meal.

One Minute Solution:
Traditional Asian etiquette dictates that you top off others' beverages, yet never your own.

Besides following tradition, your Taiwanese client is also giving you the cue that he would like you to replenish his beverage. Be sure to reciprocate.

The Art of Finger Tapping

AWKWARD SITUATION:
Wondering why your Hong Kong Chinese client has his index and middle fingers slightly bent and is lightly touching the table.

ONE MINUTE SOLUTION:
Your Hong Kong Chinese client is displaying his thanks to the server for pouring tea.

This tradition originated during the Qing Dynasty. The emperor wanted to hear the village scuttlebutt for himself, so he asked a few of the men in his court to give him laypeople's clothes. He then asked them to take him to the local teahouse where he could hear what the people in his village were discussing. He told the individuals in his court who were seated at his table not to give him away when he replenished their tea (normally they would kowtow). Instead, they were asked to honor him by lightly tapping their bent index and middle fingers, which were to resemble the kowtow. Thus, the art of finger tapping became a tradition.

Okay Nothing!

AWKWARD SITUATION:
Meeting with your Brazilian client only to have your colleague make the OK sign when you know this finger gesture is considered offensive to Brazilians.

ONE MINUTE SOLUTION:
Quickly help your colleague to recover by explaining to your Brazilian client that his gesture means "great job" in the North American culture.

The OK sign is considered perfectly acceptable and even commonplace in the United States. It is an obscene gesture, however, in many cultures outside the United States.